Rivers

by Sally Hewitt

amicus

Published by Amicus
P.O. Box 1329, Mankato, Minnesota 56002

Printed in the United States of America at Corporate
Graphics, in North Mankato, Minnesota.

Published by arrangement with the Watts Publishing
Group Ltd., London.

Library of Congress Cataloging-in-Publication Data
Hewitt, Sally.
  Rivers / by Sally Hewitt.
    p. cm. -- (Starting geography)
  Includes index.
  Summary: "Describes the geography of rivers, the
impact humans have on them, and conservation of
these areas. Also describes plant and animal life in and
around around rivers. Includes hands-on activities"--
Provided by publisher.
  ISBN 978-1-60753-128-9 (library binding)
  1. Rivers--Juvenile literature. I. Title.
  GB1203.8.H48 2011
  551.48'3--dc22
                                        2009051432

Editor: Katie Dicker
Art Direction: Dibakar Acharjee (Q2AMedia)
Designer: Shruti Aggarwal, Neha Kaul (Q2AMedia)
Picture researcher: Kamal Kumar (Q2AMedia)
Craft models made by: Tarang Saggar (Q2AMedia)
Photography: Dibakar Acharjee (Q2AMedia)

1211
32010

9 8 7 6 5 4 3 2 1

Picture credits:
t=top b=bottom c=center l=left r=right

Cover: Shutterstock.
Title page: Wonganan Sukcharoenkana/Istockphoto.
Insides: Juan Carlos Munoz/Photolibrary: 6,
Maksym Gorpenyuk/Shutterstock: 7b, Yann Arthus-
Bertrand/Corbis: 9t, Laurin Rinder/Shutterstock: 10t,
Alfgar/Shutterstock: 10b, Diego Azubel/ IndiaPicture/EPA:
12t, Bojan Brecelj/Corbis: 12b, Wonganan
Sukcharoenkana/Istockphoto: 14, Maxstockphoto/
Shutterstock: 15br, Graeme Knox/Shutterstock: 16t,
Shutterstock: 16b, Robert Ellis/Istockphoto: 18, Victoria
McCormick/Photolibrary: 19t, Tyler Olson/Shutterstock:
20t, Sergey Mostovoy/123RF: 20b, Patrick Ward/Corbis:
22t, Patrick Armstrong/Big Stock Photo: 22b, Joel W.
Rogers/Corbis: 24t, Evron/Shutterstock: 24b, Vito
Lee/Reuters: 26, Paul Glendell/Alamy: 27t, Geoffrey
Kuchera/Shutterstock: 27b. Q2AMedia Image Bank:
Imprint page, Contents page, 9, 11, 13, 15, 17, 19, 21,
23.Q2AMedia Art Bank: 7, 8, 17, 19, 25.

With thanks to our model Shruti Aggarwal.

Contents

Words that appear in
bold can be found in the
glossary on pages 28–29.

What Is a River?

A river is a wide stream of water flowing over land to the sea. Rivers flow along **channels** that can be straight or winding, wide or narrow, deep or shallow.

Longest and Biggest!

The world's longest river is the Nile River in Africa, at 4,145 miles (6,671 km) long. The Amazon River in South America is 4,002 miles (6,440 km) long. It is the second longest river, but the Amazon is the biggest since it holds the most water.

The Amazon River flows through thick rain forest, pouring 25 million gallons (94 million L) of water into the Atlantic Ocean every second!

The Water Cycle

Rivers are part of the **water cycle**. When rain falls onto the land, some soaks into the ground or is taken in by plants. Rainwater also collects in lakes and ponds and flows from streams and rivers into the ocean. When this water **evaporates**, it rises into the air where it forms clouds and falls back to the ground as rain, sleet, or snow.

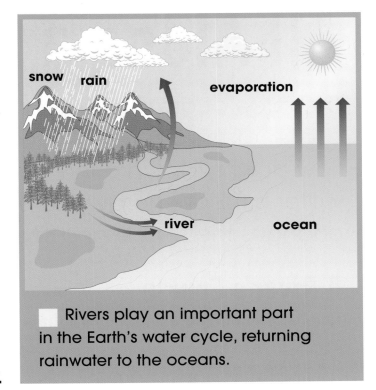

Rivers play an important part in the Earth's water cycle, returning rainwater to the oceans.

River Water

The water that flows in rivers comes from rainwater, melted snow, and natural streams called **springs**. Small streams run downhill and join together to form rivers. Smaller rivers and streams that run into a bigger river are called **tributaries**.

Mountain streams run quickly over rocks down a mountain. They join together to form a river.

All Along a River

The force of **gravity** pulls things toward the center of the Earth. This makes river water flow downhill toward the ocean. The flowing water is full of **energy** and constantly changes the shape and size of the river.

A River's Course

The route of a river is called its course. It begins in high ground at the **source**. The highest part of a river, the upper course, is narrow and fast-flowing. In the middle course, the river becomes wider and deeper. In the lower course, the river flows more slowly, curving over flat ground.

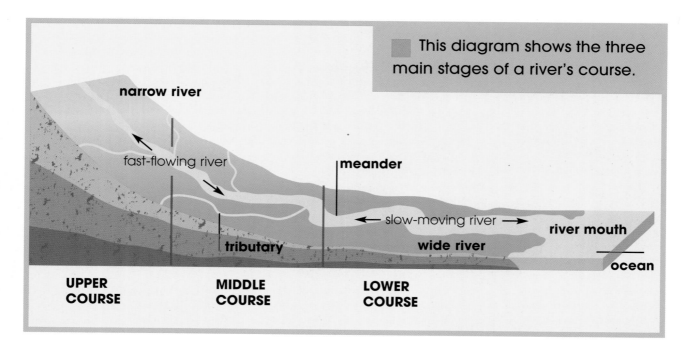

This diagram shows the three main stages of a river's course.

narrow river

fast-flowing river

meander

slow-moving river

river mouth

tributary

wide river

ocean

UPPER COURSE

MIDDLE COURSE

LOWER COURSE

A River's Mouth

The mouth of a river is where the water flows into the ocean. This area is called an **estuary**. Some rivers drop **sediment** as they reach the ocean. If the sediment splits the river into separate channels, a **delta** forms.

This river has dropped sediment as it approaches the ocean, creating a triangle-shaped delta.

Make a Model River Course

You will need:
• large rectangular tray
• self-hardening clay
• modeling tools to carve the clay • waterproof paints • jug of water

1 At one end of the tray, build a clay mountain with steep slopes at the top, gentle slopes lower down, and a flat base.

2 Carve a river course down your mountain. Make it narrow at the top and wider at the bottom.

Add clay rocks for the river to flow over.

3 Paint your river course with blue and green paints, with some white or silver specks for foam and sunlight on the water. Leave to dry.

4 Pour water slowly into the top of your river course. Watch the water follow the course down the mountain.

Wearing Away the Land

Over many years, rivers **erode** the ground they flow over. They can create deep channels called gorges or canyons, and dramatic waterfalls.

Gorges and Canyons

Erosion takes place when riverwater carries soil, sand, and loose stones. These materials scrape and carve out the banks, or sides, of the river and the riverbed or bottom. Over many years, this makes the river deeper and wider.

The Colorado River helped to form the Grand Canyon over a period of six million years.

Waterfalls

Waterfalls form in the upper course of a river, where hard and soft rock meet. The water erodes the soft rock, leaving a ledge of hard rock. The river tumbles over the ledge to make a waterfall.

This waterfall has worn away a basin beneath it called a plunge pool.

Create a Waterfall Model

Ask an adult to help you with this activity.

You will need:
- shoe box • glue or tape
- scissors • waterproof paints
- green tissue paper
- plastic (from a large sandwich bag)
- bubble wrap

1 Take the lid off the shoe box and put it over a narrow side of the box to make an L-shape. Glue or tape it in place. Ask an adult to cut the sides of the box to make it look like the edges of a riverbank.

2 Paint the box brown and green to look like rocks and plants around a waterfall. Paint the bottom (inside) green and blue for the plunge pool.

3 Cut the green tissue paper to make feathery ferns and water plants, and glue them to the inside edges of the box.

4 Cut the plastic into long ribbons and stick them to the top of the lid so they dangle down into the plunge pool and create a waterfall. You could add some bubble wrap to your pool to look like foam from the falling water.

Flood Plains

Flood plains are found along the lower course of a river, where the water flows slowly and the land on either side is flat.

Rich Farmland

When heavy rain falls, or water from melted snow flows down from the mountains, the river swells and overflows onto its flood plain. Sediment made of sand, soil, and bits of rock in the riverwater drops onto the ground, creating rich farmland.

Farmland by the Yangtze River in China is good for growing crops.

Irrigation channels bring water from the Nile River to this dry farmland.

Irrigation

The Nile River in Africa flows through areas of **desert** where it hardly ever rains. Farmers store the river water in **irrigation** channels. They use it to water their crops throughout the year.

Make a Self-Watering System

Ask an adult to help you with this activity.

You will need:

- small plastic water bottle
- duct tape • marker
- square of strong plastic about 4 x 4 in. (10 x 10 cm) (from a strong plastic bag)
- pin • rubber band
- potted plant in soil • water

1 Remove the plastic lid from the bottle. Ask an adult to cut the bottom off of the bottle and to put duct tape over the sharp edge.

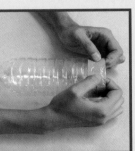

2 Trace the bottle top onto the square of plastic with the marker. Ask an adult to make four or five small holes in the plastic circle with the pin.

3 Put the plastic over the bottle top, and secure it in place with a rubber band.

4 Turn the bottle upside down and push it into the soil next to the plant you need to water. Fill the bottle with water.

Your self-watering system stores water and helps to water your plant gradually. This is particularly useful if you have to go away for a few days. You could use larger bottles for outdoor plants.

Bends and Loops

If you follow a river's course on a map, you will see that it does not travel in a straight line. As the river gets bigger, it bends and loops as the water weaves from side to side.

Meandering Along

Meanders are bends in a river. The flow of water (the current) is faster around the outside of a bend and erodes the bank. On the inside of a bend, the slower current drops sediment and makes the bend bigger.

Oxbow Lake

As the bends of a meander get bigger, they move toward each other. Sometimes, the two bends meet and the river begins to flow between them. When this happens, the bend is cut off from the river and forms an oxbow lake.

oxbow lake

The bends in a river can become so big that an oxbow lake forms.

Play "Pooh Sticks"

Play this game from the Winnie-the-Pooh books to see which parts of a river have the strongest current.

Two adults must be present during this activity at all times

You will need:
- a friend • two adults
- stopwatch

1 Visit a small river or stream near where you live, with a footbridge crossing over it.

2 Find two sticks. Push each stick through a large leaf to make them easy to recognize.

3 Mark a place about 60 feet (20 m) downstream in the direction that the current is flowing. Make sure the bridge is still visible from this position. Ask your friend and an adult to stand by the mark with a stopwatch.

4 With an adult, take the sticks to the bridge. Shout "Go!" as you drop one stick into the middle of the river and your friend starts the stopwatch.

5 How long does the stick take to reach the mark? Drop the other stick closer to the bank and do the same. Where is the current stronger? You could record your findings on a chart.

River Plants

Many different kinds of plants grow in riverbeds, along riverbanks, or in river water. Plants grow best in a slow-flowing river. A fast current may wash away soil and the plants that grow in it.

Along the Banks

Willow trees often grow along riverbanks because they need to drink plenty of water. Their roots help to stop the banks from eroding. When tall reeds grow close together by the riverbank, they provide shelter for birds and river **mammals**.

Birds often build their nests in the reeds by a riverbank.

Water lilies have flat leaves that float on the water to face the sunlight.

Plants in the Water

Some water plants keep the river water healthy and full of **oxygen**. In fast-flowing water, plants growing up from the river-bed have long, flexible stems. In slow-flowing water, some plants have flat leaves that float on the surface.

Paint a River Plant Picture

You will need:
- large sheet of paper
- several small sheets of paper • pencil • paints

1 With an adult, visit a local river (or research a river on the Internet) to learn about the plants that grow there. If you arrange a visit, you can sketch your river and the plants you see (or you could take photographs).

2 Paint a stretch of the river and the riverbanks on a large sheet of paper.

3 Paint the river plants on the small pieces of paper (or print your photographs). Use books or the Internet to find out the names of the plants.

4 Stick the plant pictures around the edge of your river painting and label them clearly. Draw arrows to show where the plants are found.

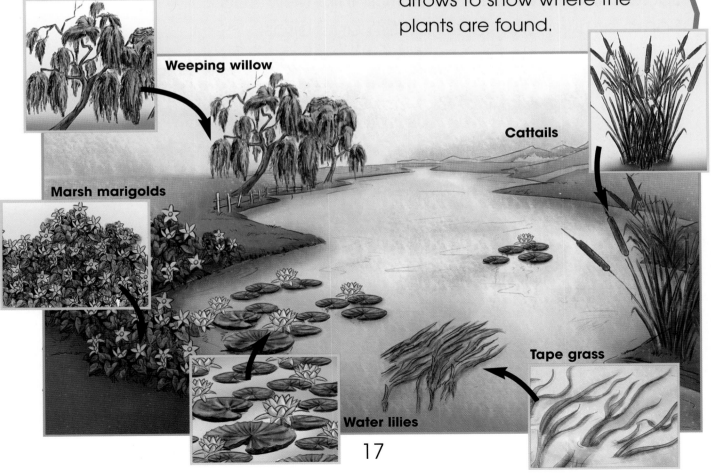

Weeping willow

Cattails

Marsh marigolds

Tape grass

Water lilies

17

River Wildlife

Rivers provide food and shelter for all kinds of animals—fish, birds, **amphibians**, **reptiles**, mammals, and insects. If there is a lot of wildlife using the river, it usually means that the water is clean and healthy.

Frogs and Toads

Frogs and toads are amphibians that live in the water and on land. You might see them swimming in the water, hopping on the bank, or sitting on a water lily leaf. They lay hundreds of eggs, called spawn, in the water that hatch into new frogs. Some spawn are eaten by fish and birds.

Frogs make their home in a river or pond. Their eggs hatch in the spring.

Mammals

Otters and beavers are river mammals. They dig their burrows in the banks of a river. Otters catch fish, frogs, and birds to eat. Beavers eat the bark from trees. They use their sharp teeth to drag branches into the water to build a dam.

Beavers build a dam to collect flowing river water. The dam makes a large, safe pool for them to swim in.

Make a Beaver Dam

You will need:
- deep rectangular tray
- rocks and sticks
- self-hardening clay • jug of water • sheet of paper
- waterproof paints

3 Pour water slowly into the smaller space behind the dam and watch it collect and form a pool.

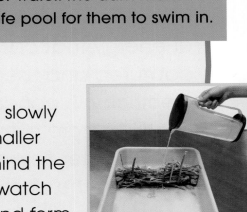

1 Build a wall with rocks and sticks, about a third of the way along the tray.

2 Use the clay to fill any gaps. Leave a small gap in the middle of the dam for the water to trickle through.

4 Paint a backdrop for your dam on the large sheet of paper, showing a forest with a family of beavers living there.

Using Rivers

People have always lived by rivers. River water can be used for drinking and for washing. Farmers use it to water their crops. A healthy river is also full of fish to eat.

Water Power

Flowing river water is full of energy that can be captured and used to make **electricity**. A concrete dam is built to store river water. Jets of water flow through spaces in the dam and turn **turbines** that help to make electricity.

Water is stored by a dam at this power station to help make electricity.

Modern factories clean their wastewater before releasing it into a river.

Factories

Many factories are built on the banks of rivers. The river water is used to help make **goods**, but the wastewater these factories produce can be full of chemicals. If it is poured back into the river, it will cause harm.

Make a Water Filter

Ask an adult to help you with this activity.

You will need:
- large plastic bottle • scissors
- duct tape • paper towel
- sand • gravel • cotton balls
- cooking oil • selection of foodstuffs (such as rice, oatmeal, and tea leaves)
- jug of water • spoon

1 Ask an adult to help you cut the plastic bottle in half and put duct tape over the sharp edge. Take off the cap.

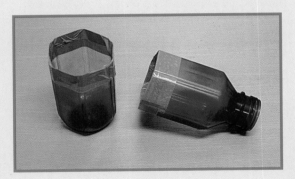

2 Put the top half of the bottle upside down into the bottom half to make a funnel. Add layers of filter materials to your funnel in the following order—a paper towel, a layer of sand, a layer of gravel, some cotton balls.

3 Add a tablespoon of cooking oil and the foodstuffs to a jug of water and stir. Pour the mixture slowly through the filter.

The filter helps to separate out some of the foodstuffs. How clean is the water that comes through the filter?

River Transportation

Rivers are natural routes that can be used to transport people and goods. Wide, deep, and very long rivers help ships and boats to travel inland. They load and unload at **ports** along the banks of the river.

Canals

Canals are man-made rivers. They were dug between towns and used to join rivers before railways became a popular form of transportation. Horses walked along **towpaths** to pull barges loaded with coal or other goods.

Barges used to be pulled along by a horse on the towpath.

Light birchbark canoes can be easily transported.

River Boats

Rivers have always been a popular place for people to settle, with transportation so close to home. Many years ago, rafts, boats, and canoes were only made from local materials. In Canada, for example, strong, light canoes were built from the soft bark of birch trees.

Make a Birchbark Canoe

You will need:
- brown thin card stock or strong paper • pencil
- scissors • hole punch
- string • cardboard • glue or tape • markers

1 Fold the card stock in half lengthwise. Draw a line 3/4 in. (2 cm) above the center fold. Fold back one side of the card stock along this line. Turn over and repeat.

2 Turn the card so the folds are along the bottom (in a kind of W-shape, but with the middle fold much shorter). Flatten and draw a canoe shape. Make sure the bottom edge of the card stock is the bottom of your canoe. Cut it out.

3 Punch four holes along each end. Thread the string through the holes and secure tightly.

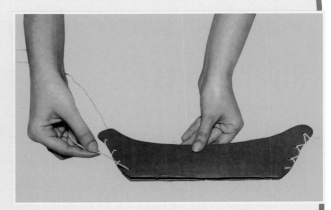

4 Push down the center fold to give your canoe a flat bottom. Cut two small strips of cardboard and tape or glue them across the top to make two seats.

5 Decorate your canoe with markers. Cut out a paddle from the cardboard to match your canoe.

Enjoying Rivers

There are lots of ways to enjoy a river, from rowing in a boat to walking along the river-bank. There are fish to catch in the water and water birds to spot in the plants and trees.

River Sports

Many people enjoy river sports to get fit and to have fun. Skilled sports include paddling canoes or rowing boats (with up to eight rowers) along straight, flat stretches of river.

In this competition, strong rowers are racing along a river.

A white water raft twists and turns along a raging river.

White Water

Rivers tumble downhill over ridges and boulders, sending up spray and foam and creating rapids or "white water." People put on life jackets and go down the rapids in rafts or canoes for a thrilling ride.

Play the Great River Race Board Game

You will need:
- large sheet of cardboard
- markers and crayons • dice
- game pieces (or you could make canoes, rafts, and boats from self-hardening clay)

1 Copy the game shown below onto the cardboard.

2 Take turns rolling the dice and moving your game pieces across the board.

3 Follow the instructions on the squares you land on. The first to get to the ocean is the winner! Can you make a river race board game of your own?

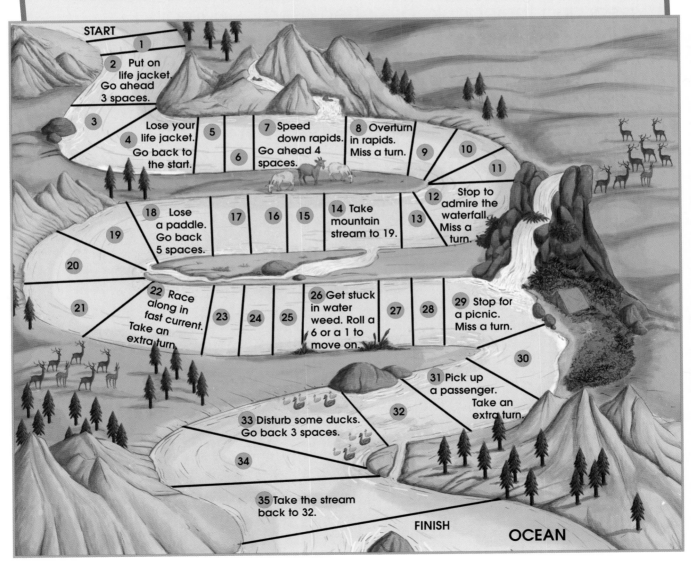

START
1
2 Put on life jacket. Go ahead 3 spaces.
3
4 Lose your life jacket. Go back to the start.
5
6
7 Speed down rapids. Go ahead 4 spaces.
8 Overturn in rapids. Miss a turn.
9
10
11
12 Stop to admire the waterfall. Miss a turn.
13
14 Take mountain stream to 19.
15
16
17
18 Lose a paddle. Go back 5 spaces.
19
20
21
22 Race along in fast current. Take an extra turn.
23
24
25
26 Get stuck in water weed. Roll a 6 or a 1 to move on.
27
28
29 Stop for a picnic. Miss a turn.
30
31 Pick up a passenger. Take an extra turn.
32
33 Disturb some ducks. Go back 3 spaces.
34
35 Take the stream back to 32.
FINISH
OCEAN

Caring for Rivers

Pollution and garbage can harm rivers and the wildlife that depends on them. If some river plants grow too thick, they stop other wildlife from growing. Everyone can get involved in keeping their local river clean and healthy.

Garbage

Rivers and their banks are often used as dumping grounds for car tires, shopping carts, traffic cones, and other garbage. Snack bags and plastic bottles thrown away carelessly can clog up the water flow and harm river wildlife.

These fish have died because their river home has become polluted.

Harmful Plants

Some river plants have been introduced from other countries. They can grow thick and tall, killing **native** plants and harming wildlife. Getting to know harmful plants and reporting them helps control their growth.

Japanese knotweed grows on U.S. riverbanks. It prevents the growth of native plants, erodes the banks, and can cause flooding.

Adopt a Local River

1 Get to know your local river and the plants and animals that live there.

2 Draw sketches or take photographs of the plants and animals that you see.

3 Find out about an organization that cares for your local river (such as www.rivernetwork.org). Join on your own, or find out if your school will get involved. Help out with one of their projects to look after a river.

Glossary

amphibian
An amphibian is an animal that lives in water and on land.

channel
A channel is a trench or groove cut into the land. River water flows along channels.

delta
A delta is a flat, swampy area of land at a river's mouth. It is made when a river drops sediment as it approaches the sea.

desert
A desert is a rocky or sandy area of land with little rainfall.

electricity
Electricity is a kind of energy made in power plants. We use electricity in our homes to turn lights on and to work machines.

energy
Energy is the power to work. River water has lots of energy.

erode
Erode means to wear away.

estuary
An estuary is the mouth of a river, where river water mixes with seawater.

evaporate
Water evaporates when it turns into a gas called water vapor.

goods
Goods are items such as food or building materials that we transport from place to place.

gravity
Gravity is a force that pulls objects toward the Earth's center.

irrigation
Irrigation is the supplying of water to crops growing in dry fields.

mammal
Mammals are animals with fur or hair. Mammal mothers feed their babies with their own milk.

native

Native plants or animals have always grown in an area and have not come from elsewhere.

oxygen

Oxygen is a gas that almost all living things need to survive.

pollution

Pollution is when something is made dirty. Riverwater can become polluted with garbage or harmful chemicals.

port

A port is a place by the coast or a riverbank where boats can load and unload people and goods.

reptile

A reptile has scaly skin and is cold-blooded. Reptiles, such as snakes and crocodiles, need heat from the sun to warm them up.

sediment

Sediment is the bits of Earth and rock carried by riverwater.

source

The source of a river is the point where it begins.

spring

A spring is where water bubbles up from underground.

towpath

A towpath is a path beside the bank of a river or canal.

tributaries

Tributaries are rivers or streams that join a bigger river.

turbines

Turbines are wheels turned by flowing water or air to make energy.

water cycle

The water on Earth goes round and round in a water cycle. Water falls as rain and runs into rivers and the sea. The water evaporates to make clouds and falls again as rain.

Index